Adventures with WORDS

by Adelaide Holl
Elementary School Teacher
Worthington, Ohio

pictures by J.P.Miller

GOLDEN PRESS • NEW YORK

distributed by

ENCYCLOPÆDIA BRITANNICA
CHICAGO

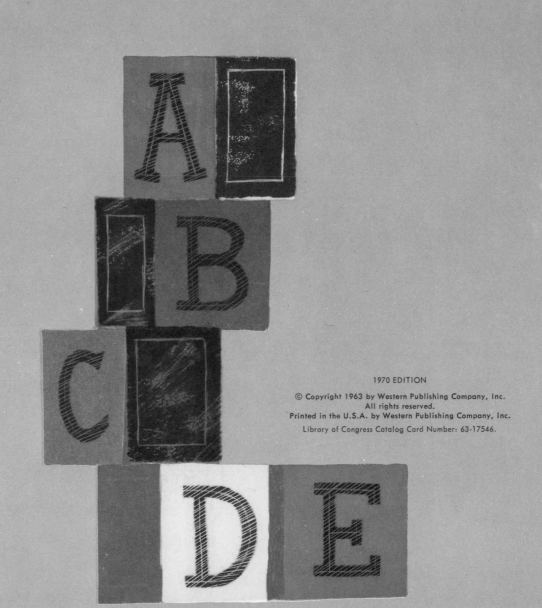

1970 EDITION

© Copyright 1963 by Western Publishing Company, Inc.
All rights reserved.
Printed in the U.S.A. by Western Publishing Company, Inc.
Library of Congress Catalog Card Number: 63-17546.

When you were a little baby, you could not talk.
You could laugh, and cry, and make funny sounds.
But you could not talk, because you could not say words.

Now, you use many words when you talk.
You say, "Good morning, Daddy,"
or "Thank you, Mother,"
or "Please pass the toast."

You use words to say, "Happy Birthday, Sally,"
or "This party is fun!"
You use words when you sing, too.

Words can tell us names for people.

Who are these people?

MR. John Smith
Jamestown
Virginia

U.S.MAIL

Can you find something
that belongs to each person?

Words can tell us names of animals, too.

Can you name these animals?

Baby animals have names, too.

Can you find their mothers
on the opposite page?

Things have names just as people and animals do.

Our house is cozy, warm, and wide.
It has the nicest things inside:

A KITCHEN where my mother cooks,
A SHELF with lots of PICTURE BOOKS,

A RUG that's soft beneath my feet,
A TABLE where we sit to eat.

For eating dinner every night
I have a PLATE that's round and white,

I have a BOWL.
I have a SPOON.
I use them for my SOUP at noon.

A KNIFE,
A FORK,
A yellow CUP
For drinking all my cocoa up.

12

We've lots of CHAIRS for sitting in.

Some chairs are fat and some are thin.

My daddy's chair is big and tall.
The one I use is rather small.

A DESK is where we sit to write.
We use a LAMP to give us light.

And there's a MIRROR on the shelf.
I look at it and see myself!

I have a WASHBOWL and a TUB
Where I can play and splash and scrub.

My COMB is pink.
My TOOTHBRUSH, red.

I have a DRESSER
And a BED.

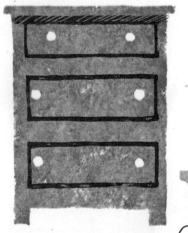

My mother tucks me in at night
And quietly turns out the light.

Outside my WINDOW I can see
The MOON and STARS shine down on me.

14

Which of these things do you have in your house?

Which of these are things your mother uses?
Which are things your daddy uses?
Which ones do you use?

Let's pretend that we are going to take a trip to the city.

Which clothes would you like to wear?

How shall we travel
to the city?

Here we are in the city.
There are many interesting places
and each one has a name.

Name the places in the picture.
Tell what you could buy in each.

Words can tell what things look like.

Here is a pet shop.
You may choose a dog of your own.
You must tell the storekeeper
exactly what your dog looks like.
Then he will know which one to give you.

Words can tell us how many.
Can you tell how many?

Let's go into a restaurant.
Choose the foods you would like.

Words can tell how things smell,
and feel, and taste.

Spicy is a word for cakes
And other things my mother bakes.

Cookies make me think of *sweet*,
And so do lots of foods I eat,
Like jelly on my breakfast toast,
And honey...I like *that* the most!

Bubbly...that's a word, I think,
That tells about some things to drink,
Like gingerale or cherry pop
Or sodas that have foam on top.

Sour is how pickles are.
My mother buys them in a jar.

Salty is for many things:
Potato chips and onion rings,
Salty peanuts, pretzels, too.
I like salty things, don't you?

Ice cream is cold and very nice.
So is water full of ice.
Soup is *hot* ...I like tomato...
Meat is hot, and baked potato.

Crispy celery's fun to chew.
So is *buttery* popcorn, too.

The different foods we have each day
Are good to eat and fun to say.

What are some foods *you* like?
Can you think of words
to tell about them?

Let's go into the toy shop.
Would you like to choose some toys?
Choose the toys you want by telling
exactly what they look like.

28

Can you find an ugly witch?
A pretty fairy?
A sad clown and a happy clown?
A fuzzy bear?
A puppet with a big red nose?

29

FLOWERS

Words can tell the colors of things.

In the flower shop we can see many plants and brightly-colored flowers.
Let's pick out a bouquet for Mother.
What colors would she like?

Here are some packets of seeds.   Can you tell what will grow from these seeds?

Plant a seed in a flower pot.   Watch it to find what happens.

Give it sunlight and water.

On our way home from the city we see many people doing many things.

We see men *building*,

children *playing*,

a farmer *working,*   and a lady *walking.*

Jump or Jiggle

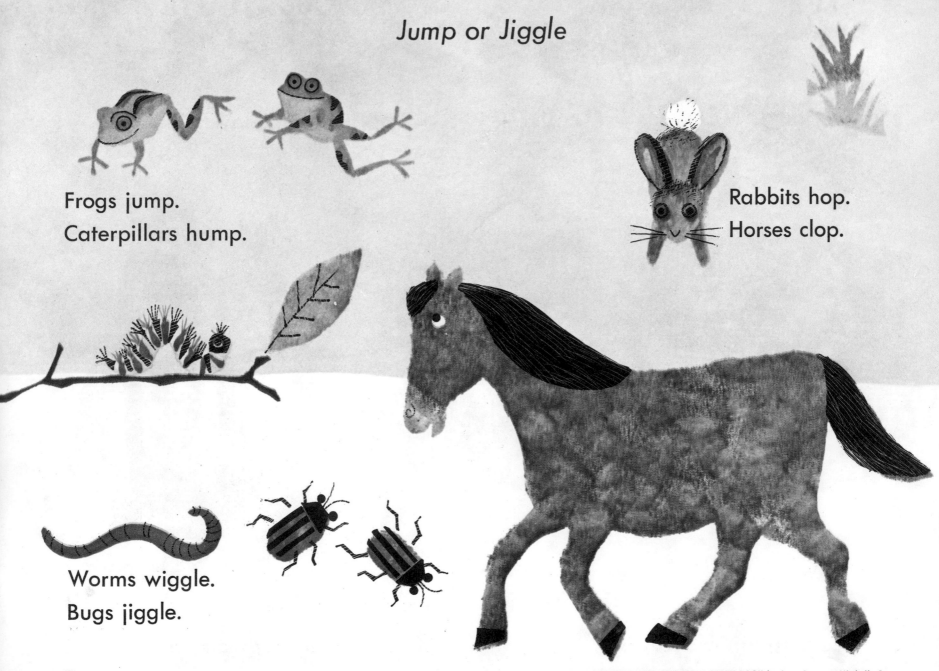

Frogs jump.
Caterpillars hump.

Rabbits hop.
Horses clop.

Worms wiggle.
Bugs jiggle.

Snakes slide.
Sea gulls glide.

Puppies bounce.
Kittens pounce.

Lions stalk—
But
I walk!

There are many words to tell about the way things move.

How many of these things can you do?

Can you climb like a squirrel?

Swing like a monkey?

Whistle like a bird?

Swim like a fish?

You can do many things that animals can not.

You can dress yourself,

and help your mother work,

and draw pictures.

Use your crayons or paints to make a picture of an animal.
What is the word that tells what your animal is doing?

37

Who is climbing *up* a ladder?

Who is standing *under* an umbrella.

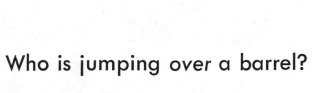

Who is jumping *over* a barrel?   Who is riding *on* a pony?

Words do not all sound alike.

Some words are loud and noisy.
These are noisy words.

BANG

BOOM

CRASH

Some words are soft and quiet.
These are soft words.

WHISPER

SLEEPY

SHHHHHHHHHH

Some words sound like something going fast.

Ker-splash!

Hippity, hop!

Some words sound like something going slow.

crawl... crawl... crawl

And some words make a rhyming sound.

cat

hat

bat

dog

frog

log

Can you think of other rhyming words?

Words do not all look alike.

There are little words.

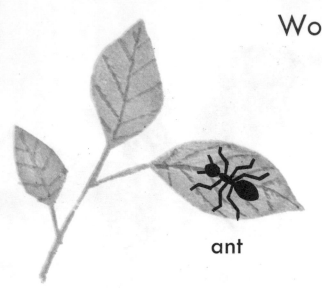

ant

bee

There are big words.

hippopotamus

rhinoceros

44

Sometimes a big animal has a little name.

ox   cow

Sometimes a little animal
has a big name.

hummingbird

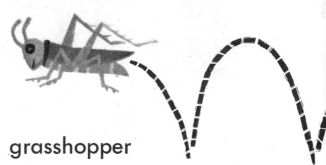

grasshopper

Words help us know what to do.

IN OUT

UP DOWN

How do these words help you know what to do?

ON
OFF

PUSH

PULL

STOP

GO

HOT   COLD

Words help Mother in her work.

They tell Daddy the news,

and they make stories fun for you.

Words are almost like magic.
We can put them together in many ways
and get all kinds of wonderful stories.

Can you guess what each of these stories
is about by looking at the picture?

Some stories are about animals.

Some stories are about real people.

And some stories are about make-believe things.

giants

dragons

witches

elves

51

Words are made up of letters.
There are 26 different letters.

Can you find the letters in your name?

When we put them together in the right way,
we have an alphabet.
The alphabet looks like this.

LMNOPQ RSTU VWXYZ

An Alphabet Rhyme

A is for airplane.
　　How swiftly it flies!
Its propellers go *hummmm!*
　　As it skims through the skies.

B is for bus
　　Going up streets and down,
Carrying passengers
　　All over town.

C is for cart.
　　Ting-a-ling! Hear the bell!
The ice-cream man's coming
　　With good things to sell.

D is for diesel.
    It zips down the track,
And all of the other cars
    Follow in back.

E is for engine
    With ladder and hose.
Eeeeee! calls the siren,
    And *whoosh!* Off it goes!

F is for ferryboat,
    Funny and slow.
Chug, chug! starts the motor!
    All aboard! Here we go!

G is for grocery truck,
    Off down the street,
Delivering all sorts
    Of good things to eat.

H is for helicopter.
    See it drop down.
The propeller on top
    Makes a *whirr-whirring* sound.

I is for iceboats.
    How lightly they go!
On runners like sleds,
    And with sails white as snow.

J is for jet
   Flying fast, flying high,
Leaving a fuzzy
   White streak in the sky.

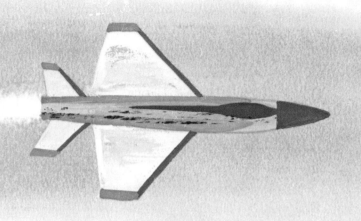

K is for kayak,
   A kind of canoe.
There is only one seat,
   So there's not room for two.

L is for lighthouse
   That stands tall and bright,
Guiding the ships
   When they travel by night.

M is for mail truck
   All red, white, and blue.
Maybe it's bringing
   A package for *you!*

N is for *Nautilus*,
   Huge submarine.
It can sail under water
   Without being seen.

O is for oil truck,
   Heavy and round.
It goes rattling along
   With a bumpety sound.

P is for parachute,
    Feathery-light.
It drifts down, down, down,
    Like a great bird of white.

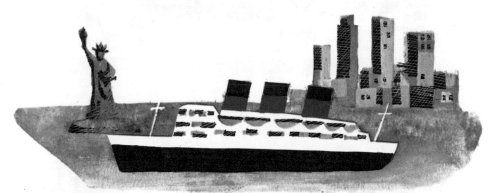

Q's for *Queen Mary.*
    She sails out the bay,
Then heads toward the ocean
    To lands far away.

R is for rocket.
    A space man's inside.
Look! There he goes
    For an orbital ride.

S is for steamboat,
    A-splashing and churning.
It puffs down the river
    With its paddle wheel turning.

T is for taxi,
    Bright yellow and black.
It takes people uptown
    And then brings them back.

U is for underground.
    Listen! Below,
With a clack and a rumble,
    The subway trains go.

V is for van—
    Someone's moving today.
When the furniture's loaded,
    It will rumble away.

W is for wagon.
    Clippity, clop!
It's all loaded with hay.
    Look who's riding on top!

X is for x-ray.
    Can *you* read the sign?
All of the people
    Are waiting in line.

Y is for yacht.
Let's go for a sail!
We might see a shark,
And we might see a whale.